Big Liam, Little Liam

Story by Ruth Morgan
Pictures by Tim Archbold

•••• dingles & company

This is the story of two boys with the same name.

Big Liam used to live with his mom in an apartment, just the two of them. His name was Liam Morden back then. He was almost taller than his mom, and he called her 'Tiny Tina'!

Little Liam Kelly used to live with his dad, Jim, in their house, just the two of them. Every Saturday night they had takeout pizza and watched the big soccer match on television.

Then Liam Morden's mom met Liam Kelly's dad. They fell in l-o-v-e (the boys didn't like saying that word out loud), and they got married. Everyone was happy except for one thing: Liam Morden became Liam Kelly.

Now there were two Liam Kellys and they didn't even look like brothers!

Having two Liams in the same house caused problems.

In the morning Tiny Tina would shout upstairs, "Hey, Liam. Do you need your soccer equipment today?"

"Yes, please," one Liam would shout.

"No thanks!" shouted the other Liam.

Tiny Tina got very confused!

The worst time was Christmas. Some presents just had "To Liam" written on them.

"Mine!" one Liam would shout.

"No, mine!" shouted the other Liam.

It was like tug of war but not as friendly.

Sometimes it was easy to tell which present was which!

Why couldn't each Liam be called something a little different?

Tiny Tina wanted to call them "Liam One" and "Liam Two", but the boys didn't like that.

Jim wanted to call them "Big Liam" and "Little Liam", but the boys didn't like that either.

So they were both called just "Liam", and sometimes that was confusing.

One morning, Jim was making scrambled eggs on toast.

"You don't like scrambled eggs, do you Liam?" Jim asked.

"Yuck, no thanks," said one Liam.

"You know I do," said the other Liam.

Jim was very confused.

Both Liams read the back of the cornflakes box. There was a competition. You had to paint a picture of a dragon, and the first prize was any bike you wanted!

"I saw the competition first!" Liam shouted, pulling at the box.

"No, I did," shouted the other Liam.

"Look, boys," said Jim. "You are both good at painting. You can both enter the competition."

"Okay," they both said.

Liam went into the living room to do his painting. He didn't want anyone to see. He painted a red dragon with webbed wings. The only part of his painting he didn't like was the legs. He just couldn't get them to look right.

The other Liam went up to the bedroom to do his painting. He didn't want anyone to see. He painted a green dragon with long legs. The only part of his painting he didn't like was the wings. He tried painting them again and again, but they still looked like serving trays!

The boys met on the stairs.

"Have you finished your painting?" asked Liam.

"Nearly," said Liam. "What about you?"

"Um…nearly," said Liam.

"Do you think you're going to win?"

"Do you?"

"No."

"No. Neither do I."

Both boys looked fed up.

"There's something wrong with
my dragon. Take a look," said
Liam. "Its legs just aren't right. I've
tried and tried, but I can't make
them look any better."

"The rest of it is good," said Liam.
"I like the wings. I can't paint wings at all.
Look at these things like serving trays on mine!"

Both boys laughed.

"Hey, I have an idea," said Liam.
"How about if I paint your dragon's
wings…"

"…and I paint your dragon's
legs!" said Liam. "What a great
idea!"

"Don't tell anyone, though."

"I won't if you won't!"

So off they went to help each
other out. They were busy
painting for the rest of the
morning.

Later that day, they went to the
post office and mailed a big envelope
off to the cornflakes competition.

"I hope you're lucky," said one
Liam with a smile.

"I hope you are, too." The other
Liam smiled back.

One morning two months later, the boys were having breakfast. Jim ran into the kitchen with a letter in his hand.

"I think it's about the cornflake competition," he said.

Tiny Tina read the name on the envelope. She stopped smiling.

"It says *To Liam Kelly*," she said. "Which one do they mean?"

"You'd better open it," said one of the Liams.

Tiny Tina opened the envelope
slowly. She read the letter.
"You've won," she gasped.
"Well, one of you has. It says
that Liam Kelly has won first
prize in the dragon
painting competition."
Jim looked worried.
The boys smiled at
each other.

17

Tiny Tina went on reading. She looked very worried, too.

"We would like Liam Kelly to come to the Town Hall on Friday, April 13th, at 11.00 a.m. He will be given an award and asked to pick the bike he wants as his prize!"

"Friday the 13th!" gasped Jim. "That's unlucky."

Things were getting worse and worse.

"Who's going to go?" asked Jim.

"Who's going to go?" asked Tiny Tina.

"Liam and I had better both go," said one Liam.

"We'd all better go," said the other.

Over the next few weeks, Jim tried to talk to his son.

"Will you be very upset if you don't win?" asked Jim.

"I'll hit the roof," said Liam. "I want to win more than anything in the world."

But when Jim left the room, Liam smiled to himself.

Over the next few weeks, Tiny Tina tried to talk to her son.

"If you don't win..." she said.

"Don't say it, Mom," said Liam. "If I don't win I'll go bananas. I'll never talk to Liam ever again!"

But when she left the room, Liam smiled to himself.

Poor Jim and Tiny Tina! They were worried that the two Liams would stop being friends. They didn't know what to do.

On Friday, April 13th, the Kelly family arrived at the Town Hall. They sat down in the front row, near the stage.

The judge named everyone who had won third and second prizes in the competition.

"But guess who has won first prize," he said.

Then he held up a wonderful painting of two flying dragons, one red and one green, with long legs and webbed wings.

"The winner is Liam Kelly!" he said.

Both Liams looked at each other. Then they stood up and walked to the stage together.

"We're both Liam Kelly," the boys told the judge. "We both painted the picture together, and we know what kind of bike we want as our prize."

"Congratulations!" laughed the judge. "Name your bike!"

23

A week later the bike arrived, with a photographer to take a picture for the newspaper.

The bike was a tandem, a bike made for two people!

Big Liam rode in front first, and the boys agreed they would always take turns. And they did!